D1507566

ERNIE LOMBARDI

PETE ROSE

GEORGE WRIGHT

BARRY LARKIN

WILL WHITE

EDD ROUSH

JOE MORGAN

EPPA RIXEY

ERIC DAVIS

FRANK ROBINSON

JOHNNY BENCH

KEN GRIFFEY JR.

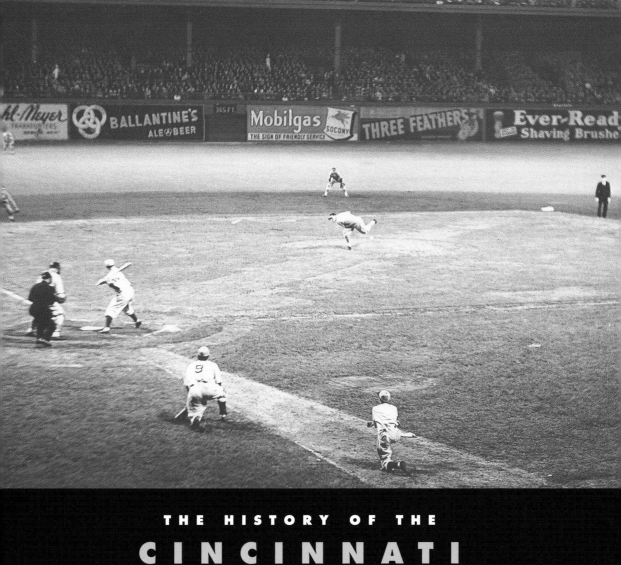

THE HISTORY OF THE

CINCINNATI
REDS

WAYNE STEWART

CREATIVE 🍎 EDUCATION

Published by Creative Education, 123 South Broad Street, Mankato, MN 56001

Creative Education is an imprint of The Creative Company.

Designed by Rita Marshall.

Photographs by AllSport (Harry How, Ronald Martinez, Rick Stewart, Matthew Stockman),

Associated Press/Wide World Photos, FotoSport (Mitch Reibel), National Baseball Library,

Anthony Neste, SportsChrome (Jeff Carlick, Rob Tringali Jr., Michael Zito)

Library of Congress Cataloging-in-Publication Data

Stewart, Wayne, 1951- The history of the Cincinnati Reds / by Wayne Stewart.

p. cm. — (Baseball)   ISBN 1-58341-205-0

Summary: A team history of the organization that is the oldest professional club in

baseball, formed in 1869.

1. Cincinnati Reds (Baseball team)—History—

Juvenile literature. [1. Cincinnati Reds (Baseball team)—History.

2. Baseball—History.] I. Title. II. Baseball (Mankato, Minn.).

GV875.C65 S84 2002   796.357'64'0977178—dc21   2001047863

First Edition 9 8 7 6 5 4 3 2 1

CINCINNATI

IS A BUSTLING CITY LOCATED IN THE SOUTHERN PART OF

Ohio. The city was founded in 1788 along the Ohio River and soon

became one of America's busiest inland water ports. It also became

a key stop as the United States expanded westward in the 1800s.

In fact, by 1850, when the phrase "Go west, young man" was first

uttered, "west" actually meant Cincinnati.

Nestled along the shore of the Ohio River in Cincinnati over

the years were two baseball stadiums and treasured landmarks:

first Crosley Field, and then Riverfront Stadium. Those stadiums

were home to the city's beloved professional baseball team, the

Reds. Formed in 1869, the Reds franchise is the granddaddy of all

professional baseball teams. In fact, for many years, no team in

GEORGE WRIGHT

baseball could begin its season before the Reds did.

{A PERFECT TEAM} The Reds were founded by businessman

Harry Wright, who decked his players out in red

uniforms. For this, the club soon became known as the

Red Stockings. Wright put together a great lineup by

assembling some of the top players from the East Coast.

Among these stars was Wright's brother George,

In history's first pro baseball game (in **1869**), Cincinnati beat the Mansfield Independents, 48–14.

a shortstop. George was awesome in the team's first season, batting

.629 and scoring a whopping 339 runs. For his sensational play,

he earned $2,000, while the rest of the team made a total of

about $9,000.

During that 1869 season, the Reds rattled off an incredible

57 wins in a row and finished the season undefeated. In fact, they

wouldn't lose until the following season when their streak had

extended to a staggering 81 victories. There was no official league in

BRETT TOMKO

Outfielder Edd Roush posted the NL's top batting average in both **1917** and **1919**.

EDD ROUSH

those days, so the Reds traveled around the country playing any team that wanted to challenge them. That changed in 1876, when the team officially became the Reds and helped to form the National League (NL) along with seven other pro teams.

The Reds' first star pitcher after joining the NL was Will White, who still holds the league record for the most starts in a season. White took the mound 75 times as a starter in 1879, a feat made possible by the effortless, underhand throwing style used by pitchers of that era. He won 43 games in 1879, still a team high.

{THE MODERN ERA BEGINS} In the early 1900s, the Reds boasted such stars as outfielder Cy Seymour, a superb hitter who batted .377 in 1905. Cincinnati also had future Hall-of-Famer Edd Roush roaming center field. In 1921, Roush struck out just

BOB BESCHER

The Reds have en-tertained fans with their hustling style for more than 130 years.

POKEY REESE

eight times, a team record that will almost certainly never be

broken. (Today it's not uncommon to see players strike out around

Cincinnati's great pitching staff surrendered an average of only 2.23 runs a game in **1919**. 150 times a season.)

By 1912, the Reds left the ballpark known as the

Palace of the Fans and began playing in a new park

later named Crosley Field. It was there that Cincinnati

won the 1919 NL pennant. The team's top three

pitchers—Slim Sallee, Hod Eller, and Dutch Ruether—were

spectacular, winning a combined 60 games that season. Cincinnati

then went on to win the World Series over the American League

champion Chicago White Sox.

That World Series was tainted, however, when some of

Chicago's players later admitted they weren't trying to win.

They had accepted bribes from gamblers to throw the series, or

make enough mistakes to lose on purpose. "One thing that's always

EPPA RIXEY

been overlooked in this whole mess is that we could have beaten

them no matter what the circumstances," Roush said of the scandal.

"The 1919 Reds were better."

{LOMBARDI LEADS THE WAY} In the 1920s, an outstanding

pitcher named Eppa Rixey arrived in Cincinnati. Rixey blew away

opposing batters to win 25 games in 1925, more than any other NL pitcher. He went on to win 266 games over the course of his stellar

big-league career, an achievement that earned him a place in the

In **1935**, the
first night
game in
major-league
history was
played at
Cincinnati's
Crosley Field.
Baseball Hall of Fame.

During the 1930s, the Reds featured a superb

catcher named Ernie Lombardi. Lombardi was one of

the slowest runners in the history of the game, yet he

still managed to win two batting crowns and finished

14 with a career .306 batting average. He readily acknowledged his lack

of speed. "In Cincinnati, I once hit the left-field wall and they threw

me out at first," Lombardi recalled.

In 1939, Lombardi, ace pitcher Bucky Walters, and hard-hitting

first baseman Frank McCormick led the Reds to their first pennant

in 20 years. Unfortunately, after going 97–57 during the regular

season, the Reds lost in the World Series, swept in four games by

the New York Yankees.

DMITRI YOUNG

In 1940, however, Cincinnati came back stronger than ever and

captured the NL pennant again. In the World Series, Walters and

pitcher Paul Derringer each won two games as the Reds outlasted

the Detroit Tigers in seven games to win the world championship.

{THE REDS RISE AGAIN} Cincinnati faded in the NL standings

in the late 1940s but assembled a powerful lineup again in the

1950s. In 1956, the Reds experienced a power surge, smacking an NL-record 221 home runs. Leading the way that year was rookie outfielder Frank Robinson, who led the league in runs scored and swatted 38 homers, a major-league rookie record that would stand for 31 years.

Before he hung up his cleats, Robinson hit 586 career homers, a total surpassed by only four players (Hank Aaron, Babe Ruth, Willie Mays, and Barry Bonds). "I don't see anyone playing in the major leagues today who combines both the talent and the intensity that I had," said the ever-confident Robinson when he was inducted into the Hall of Fame.

The Reds roared to another NL pennant in 1961. Robinson led the way at the plate, and pitchers Joey Jay and Bob Purkey led the way on the mound. Unfortunately, the Reds could not bring home another world title, losing to the Yankees and star outfielder

Slow but steady Reds catcher Ernie Lombardi was an NL All-Star every season from **1936** to **1940**.

ERNIE LOMBARDI

Today's Reds hope to rise to the heights attained by the franchise in **the 1970s**.

Mickey Mantle in the World Series.

Throughout the 1960s, the Reds' finest pitcher was Jim Maloney,

Pete Rose set many club records dur- ing his Reds career, includ- ing the most extra-base hits (868). who fired three no-hitters during the decade. Over that same 10-year period, the Reds churned out three Rookie of the Year award winners. Among them was the man that many consider the greatest catcher ever: Johnny Bench. Reds manager Sparky Anderson knew

just how special Bench was. "I don't want to embarrass any other catcher by comparing him with Johnny Bench," Anderson once said.

Still, it was second baseman Pete Rose, the 1963 Rookie of the Year, who became the most famous Reds player of that era and of all time. "He is Cincinnati," Anderson said of Rose. "He's the Reds." Known as "Charlie Hustle," Rose always played all-out, even sprinting down the first-base line when he drew a walk. His hustle and intensity won the adoration of Reds fans and earned him 13

PETE ROSE

All-Star Game appearances.

{THE "BIG RED MACHINE"} When the Reds left Crosley Field

for the brand-new Riverfront Stadium in 1970, a dynasty was just

around the corner. Once Sparky Anderson came on board as the

team's manager, the victories began to pile up in Cincinnati. Then,

when such stars as second baseman Joe Morgan were added to the mix, the pennants poured in. As the powerful Reds destroyed one

opponent after another, the media dubbed their awesome lineup

the "Big Red Machine."

By that point, Bench, who would eventually play

in 14 All-Star Games and win 10 Gold Glove awards

for his great defense, was a true superstar. In 1970,

the 22-year-old catcher smashed 45 home runs and

22 became the youngest player ever to win the NL Most Valuable

Player (MVP) award.

And then there was Morgan, the team's spark plug. With

tremendous speed and great power for a man just 5-foot-7, he was

a whirlwind. During his Reds career, he hit as many as 27 homers in a

season and twice stole as many as 67 bases. For his stellar play, he

won back-to-back NL MVP awards in 1975 and 1976. "A good base

stealer should make the whole infield jumpy," Morgan said as he

JOE MORGAN

Perhaps the greatest catcher of all time, Johnny Bench spent 17 seasons in Cincinnati.

JOHNNY BENCH

explained his base-stealing prowess. "Whether you steal or not,

you're changing the rhythm of the game."

It was the dynamic Rose, however, who was the

primary fuel that powered the Big Red Machine. Over

the course of his 20-year career, he set new major-

league records for total hits, singles, at-bats, and games

played. He also made a name for himself as one of the

most hard-nosed and passionate players of all time. "If you play an

aggressive, hustling game, it forces your opponents into errors,"

he explained.

The Reds won pennants in 1970 and 1972, but the 1975 season

was especially sweet. That year, with other great players such as

outfielder George Foster and infielders Tony Perez and Dave

Concepcion in the lineup, the Reds toppled the Boston Red Sox in

the World Series. Some baseball historians consider the 1975 Reds

First baseman Tony Perez drove in 109 runs to help the Reds win the World Series in **1975**.

TONY PEREZ

the greatest team in major-league history. Combined, the players on

that squad won six NL MVP awards, earned 26 Gold Glove awards,

and made 63 All-Star Game appearances.

This awesome lineup went 102–60 and repeated as champs

in 1976, not losing a single game in the NL Championship Series

(NLCS) or the World Series. The "Great Eight" (a nickname

bestowed on Cincinnati's regular eight batters) had led the Reds to the first back-to-back world championships by an NL team in more than 50 years.

{TO THE MILLENNIUM AND BEYOND} The Big Red Machine was dismantled over the next few seasons, and the Reds went through some lean years. Rose delighted the home crowd by smacking his big-league record 4,192nd hit in a 1984 game and then becoming the Reds' manager, but Cincinnati was no longer a powerhouse.

Shortstop Barry Larkin won fans over with his sure glove, committing just 10 errors in **1989**.

In the 1980s, new talent began arriving. Among these players was Cincinnati native Barry Larkin, a standout shortstop and fan favorite. Also emerging as a star was outfielder Eric Davis, known for his great speed and energy. "I'm supposed to steal bases," he said, explaining his reckless playing style. "I'm supposed to hit home runs. I've run into walls. I've jumped over walls to make catches."

BARRY LARKIN

The Reds moved up in the standings in the late 1980s, but

Cincinnati fans were dealt a crushing blow in 1989 when it was

Tom Browning,
the only
Reds pitcher
to ever throw
a perfect
game, won
15 games
in **1990**.

reported that Rose, the team's manager, was involved

in a gambling scandal. Even though Rose denied

charges that he had bet on baseball games, including

those played by his own team, he was banned from

the game for life, which meant that he could never

take his rightful place in the Hall of Fame.

But just when Cincinnati fans needed a lift, the Reds gave it to

them. In 1990, the team won its first nine games and never let up,

winning the NL Western Division with a 91–71 record. The Reds

then powered their way to the World Series, where outfielder Billy

Hatcher went 9-for-12 and led Cincinnati to a stunning sweep of

the mighty Oakland Athletics. "No one gave us much of a chance,"

said hard-throwing Reds pitcher Jose Rijo, who won two games in

TOM BROWNING

the series, "but we believed in ourselves and proved to everybody

we deserve to be champs."

The Reds won their division again in 1995 but

were eliminated in the divisional playoffs. In the

seasons that followed, they added a number of new

stars, including first baseman Sean Casey, outfielder

Dmitri Young, and pitchers Pete Harnisch and Danny

Outfielder Deion Sanders, who doubled as a pro football star, racked up 56 steals in **1997**.

Graves. Larkin also continued to play well, but Cincinnati could not   **29**

get back to the playoffs.

In 2000, Cincinnati made a major move by acquiring All-Star

center fielder Ken Griffey Jr. One of the top sluggers in the game,

Griffey was only 31 years old when he joined the Reds but had

already hit 438 career home runs. "Every mistake I throw, [he] hits

a home run," said Yankees pitcher David Cone. "That doesn't seem

fair. He can at least mix in a double every once in a while."

DEION SANDERS

First baseman Sean Casey batted .332 in **1999**, his first full big-league season.

SEAN CASEY

One of the game's greats, Ken Griffey Jr. combined speed, agility, and power.

KEN GRIFFEY JR.

Over the years, the Reds have built a tradition that few baseball

teams can match. The franchise boasts a history of more than

The Reds
hoped to get
an offensive
boost from
outfielder Juan
Encarnacion in
the years
ahead.

130 years, five world championships, and a lengthy

list of baseball greats that includes Edd Roush,

Frank Robinson, Johnny Bench, and Ken Griffey Jr.

Cincinnati fans eagerly await the day when the Reds—

the granddaddy of them all—once again reign as

32   baseball's world champs.

JUAN ENCARNACION